RU
LOOKING?

R U
LOOKING?

A Guide to Navigating Gay Dating

SELRACH SMITH

iUniverse, Inc.
Bloomington

R U Looking?
A Guide to Navigating Gay Dating

Author Credits: Aaron Smith

iUniverse books may be ordered through booksellers or by contacting:

iUniverse
1663 Liberty Drive
Bloomington, IN 47403
www.iuniverse.com
1-800-Authors (1-800-288-4677)

ISBN: 978-1-4759-7456-0 (sc)
ISBN: 978-1-4759-7457-7 (ebk)

Library of Congress Control Number: 2013902814

Printed in the United States of America

iUniverse rev. date: 02/28/2013

Table of Contents

Introduction

In my opinion, I live in one of the greatest cities in the world. New York, New York! This city has many nicknames: "Parade Town," "the city that never sleeps," and "the Big Apple" being the most common. One of my favorite playwrights, Stephen Sondheim, wrote a song for the play *Company* called "Another Hundred People." The songs calls New York City "a city of strangers," and I have to admit, for the most part, this is an accurate description when it comes to meeting people. On one of my many visits here during my early twenties, something happened to me that felt like it was a scene from a movie.

It was a Sunday night in October 2004, and I was at the famous Stonewall Bar in the West Village. There was a drag-queen show, a strip contest, and a drunken straight girl. Just my luck—the drunken girl bumped into me, and I was pushed into the guy next to me and spilled my drink all over him. I was so embarrassed; then I looked at him and realized he was quite attractive. I apologized and offered him another drink. A conversation started, and the next thing I knew, I was in love. That was the beginning of my first serious relationship in the "city of strangers."

So I like to believe that love brought me to New York City. However, it ended, and I was back on the singles' market three years later. Boy, did the definition of being single change a lot! I felt like the whole world had changed during the course of my relationship, and all the rules of the dating game had changed as well. I noticed a lot of people putting on acts or fronts, pretending to act like what they thought a New Yorker should be.

When you're a gay man dating in a city this big, it's almost impossible to find someone who's not trying to follow the "in-crowd" like Wall Street cattle. I'm mainly referencing the people who are doing things simply because "everyone is doing it." Take circuit parties, for example. They're a lot of fun and feature a lot of great music, nice venues, and cool people from all over, but, in my opinion, many of these parties seem to automatically invite an environment of drug use. Now don't get me wrong, you can attend a circuit party and see many people who are high as a kite and appear to be having a great time. You have to wonder what goes though one's mind when seeing this for the first time. *Maybe I should try it. He looks like he doesn't have a care in the world. Should I give him a sandwich?* I find that a lot of people try "party favors" based solely on the idea that it will allow them to have a great time and because *other people are doing it*, hence my Wall Street cattle reference. Therefore, how do you find the guys who don't fall into the Gay cliché?

So what's a "girl" to do? Do you think to yourself: I'm young, relatively attractive, health-conscious, and goal-oriented? Then you find yourself sitting at home on a weekend and asking yourself, "What the hell I am I doing? I'm a sexy, single guy in a city of eight million people." Has someone asked you this irritating question: "So why are you single?" We've all been there . . . unless you're "gaymous" or something. (Gaymous = kind-of-famous gays.)

At times I feel like I've dated half of the Gay male population in New York City. You can't turn a corner or walk down an avenue without running into someone you dated or had a late encounter with. I can also count on one hand the people I've dated outside of Manhattan. (Yes, I took a chance on love through a tunnel.) Yet I kept dating and dating and trying to keep an open mind about the type of guys I would date. Four years later, I was still single. So something had to change. It was important for me not to give up on the thought that there was someone special out there just for me. (Yes, I know what you're thinking: I'm a hopeless romantic.) Everything in this book is a result of some of my experiences and those of my friends here in this city of cities.

This book talks about the obstacles I've faced while being single and dating in New York City. We will talk about self-reflecting, how to meet people, and controlling our tendencies to fast-forward into relationships too quickly. I also want to send a message to other Gay men like me who are frustrated with all of the ups and downs of dating in any big city. I've learned a lot of lessons while being single and made many mistakes in dating. Through it all, I believe a truly wise person not only learns from his own mistakes but also learns from others. That's what I hope to accomplish here. I want Gay single men to read and learn from some of my observations.

I realize that I've made many mistakes over the years, but I try never to make the same mistake twice. So, as close friends of mine were coming out of their long-term relationships and back on the singles' market, I saw them making a lot of the same dumb-ass mistakes I did. As the pushy and evil but sweet friend that I am, I'd stop them from running into the same brick wall I repeatedly hit years ago. In several discussions with friends, I found I was repeating myself over and over, so as a joke, I said, "I'm-a write this shit down and pass it out so you will stop calling me." That's when it hit me: I'm sure my message can help other Gay men out there with this crazy world of Gay dating.

I also soon realized in my travels to other countries and other large cities that this wasn't a problem specifically related to New York City. Gay men everywhere are dealing with the same issues when it comes to dating: the cheating, the insecurities, self-hating activities, drug use. I want to help try to filter through all of that.

With this book, I hope to help some people avoid unneeded heartache and frustration. Life is filled with enough stresses, like employment, education, finances, fixing your hair, a sale at Saks. I would like whoever reads this book to picture it as an open discussion between close friends, giving some honest—but in some cases a bit harsh—advice. It all comes from a loving place in my little black-sequined heart.

> "I still believe in man.
> A wise one asked me why.
> 'Cause I just don't believe we're wicked.
> I know that we sin, but I do believe we try,"
> Ocean,Frank "We All Try" Lyrics. Nostalgia, Ultra
> Self-Release Mixtape, February 18, 2011

The lyric above is from one of my favorite songs written by Frank Ocean, called "We All Try." At one point, I wanted to give up on dating altogether. I was starting to believe there are only a few guys like me left—hopeless romantics. After many disappointments, I feel like the song above. I still believe in man too. You should never give up on what you feel you deserve. *Never* just settle for what is in front of you. Always want the *best*!

The hard part is getting people to believe that they deserve the best in the first place; I will touch on that in the book as well. I'm hoping this book starts a journey of self-discovery that will ultimately lead to smart and successful dating in any city. Let's get started.

Chapter One

DECIDE WHAT YOU WANT

What do you want out of life? Where do you see yourself in five years? (This is a favorite question of mine.) This is the first place we should start when it comes to deciding what we want. We will be asking ourselves these types of questions later in the chapter. Have you ever heard the phase "The blind leading the blind"? I see this lot with Gay men when they date. Neither person has any idea of what they want for themselves. So, how will you know if the person you're dating is the kind of man you want to be with if you don't know what you want? Ultimately knowing how to figure out what you want in life will help you when it comes to dating.

I want you to ask people around you the same questions from above. "What do you want?" and listen to each answer. This can be anyone, Friends, Family, Co-workers etc. For the most part, you'll get an "I don't know," or you'll hear a lot of people mentioning career goals. A few really smart people will hit the nail on the head and speak about things that they are passionate about. (Hint)

Now let's take a moment or several moments and put this all into perspective and find the answer to these questions. When I say *a moment,* this could be a day, a week, a month, or as long as you need. A deep self-assessment is needed to really know what you want in life. It's important for us to always know what we want so we make a plan to go and get it.

Here's one way to start. Think about those nights when you're in bed alone, and you have too many thoughts running through your head. Most of the time, this is your subconscious running in circles about work, family, or money, or what you've forgotten to do. Some of these thoughts could be issues you are trying to avoid and have a way of creeping up at some point.

A lot of people look to others to tell them the truth about themselves or about a situation. Most of the time, the truth is right in front of you. When you're lying in bed alone at night, try to stop the wheel in your brain from turning. Ask yourself some questions, and you will be surprised how the answers to your problems will just come to you. It's important to be honest with yourself when asking these questions. There's nothing worse than lying to yourself about anything. With that in mind, here are a few questions you can honestly ask yourself:

1. What do you want in general in life?

This can be anything your heart desires. Don't be afraid to explore whatever brings you joy in life. If it helps, make a list of what you want, so it can be a physical thing to hold in your hand. I've listed mine below.

Selrach's List—This is just an example of a list off the top of my head just so you can get the picture, but I always write down the things I want to do and then make a plan to figure out how to accomplish them:

1. I want a rich man (kidding).
2. I want a stable, healthy, loving, long-term relationship.
3. I want live a healthy lifestyle.
4. I want to run my own business.
5. I want to be a *New York Times* bestseller.
6. I want to volunteer to help Gay youth.
7. I want to go to the Olympics in Rio! (Okay, fine. I do not want to go to the Olympics, but, I want to be in the middle of the Olympic village, naked, covered in honey. Then I woke up from my dream.)

2. Where do you see yourself in your career in three to five years?

Most people speak about this area of life when describing themselves, but your career does not define you as a person, although having career objectives is a very attractive trait. If we get this out of the way, we can move on to what is really important.

3. What are some of your financial goals?

Finances can be a motivating thing for some people or a very stressful thing to others. For the average person money problems can create a lot of stress, but having some type of plan to put yourself in a better place is a way to keep your thoughts off this. Also, having money related issues when dating can be a problem. (Hell, if you can't pay for dinner, then you need to keep your happy ass at home. ☺) Seriously, if you're having financial troubles, the best thing to do is stay home! Then go online and educate yourself on everything related to your money! Review all bank and credit-card statements and make sure you know what your interests rates are for everything. I'm not going to go into how to fix some of these issues, but at the very least understand your current situation so you can make smart decisions to fix it. If you're on the other end of these things, then this is not a concern for you.

4. What will help you to be a better person?

Part of your answer to this question should have come from the first question. If it didn't, that's fine too. There is no right or wrong answer to this question. Only an individual can determine what will make him a better person, but self-improvement in any form is always attractive.

Start by finding out exactly where you are in life. Stand in front of a mirror and ask yourself a few questions that start with "Am I happy with my . . . ." Possible topics are: health, fitness, money, family issues, hair, sex life, dating, myself. Regardless of these answers, it's important to know where you currently stand. Only then can you begin to put some things in order. Don't be afraid to ask close friends their opinions on these things about you. I do not recommend relying on others' opinions, but sometimes people on the outside can give you a different point of view, one you were not aware of.

5. What makes life worth living?

This answer will be different for everyone, but personally I think whatever inspires you or allows you to just clear your mind of all thoughts is what makes life worth living. It can be something very simple really. I remember being around 7 or 8 years old and just lying in the grass in the backyard staring at the sky. I didn't have a care in the world just looking at the clouds. Today I think back to that time and remember how peaceful that was. So even as an adult when I see something in nature that's beautiful I have to stop and appreciate it. The funny thing is life gets so crazy we forget to do these little things to remind us of what brings us peace.

6. What you will not deal with?

This question is a trip, but trust me—when looking for your future partner, it's important to know what you will stand for so you will not take any crap from anyone.

For me, r-e-s-p-e-c-t! This is very important to me. (It's also one of the first words I learned to spell, thanks to Aretha Franklin.) I believe in respecting everyone, but the minute I'm disrespected, I lose my mind, and it's not a pretty sight. In my opinion, respect is a basic requirement we all deserve. We also need to respect ourselves first. So if I'm on a date with someone I've been talking to for a while, and he turns and gawks at some random guy while we are talking . . . well, let's just say a hot baked potato will be flying across the table. That's not the *best* way to handle that situation, but just make a mental note of what kind of person you're dealing with and decide if that is something you can tolerate.

7. Are you emotionally ready for a relationship?

Okay, this is your first moneymaker right here! Most of us have turmoil from our childhood and other areas of life that we have not dealt with. Like why the hell did your mom send you to school with those damn penny loafers (with the penny in it) when you wanted a pair of Nikes? Seriously, this is a very important question that must be answered honestly. What I'm about to mention is a very common mistake many people make. *Do not get into a relationship as a solution to your emotional issues.* Sam Dees wrote a song that was originally recorded by the Manhattans. In 1987, Whitney Houston recorded the same song, called "Just the Lonely Talking Again." The chorus of the song asks, "Tell me, are you really ready for love, boy? Or is it just the lonely talking again?"

I have been guilty of this lyric many times until I woke up and realized this was not the way to go, and I told the "lonely" to shut up. I think Gay men in general tend to be lonely people. We have to learn to enjoy our own company and be content with ourselves before we can try to bring someone into our life.

I've also dated guys who were badly damaged emotionally by exes or others and never dealt with what happened to them. Instead, they took the easy path and moved on to the next guy, even though they were just creating a ticking bomb by hiding these issues. It's like hitting your head against a brick wall. Even with the blood running down our faces, we keep repeating ourselves. (I think they call that insanity . . . . Just saying.)

This is not the answer to your emotional issues. We all have them, but if these things are not addressed, you should put this book down and deal with them before moving forward. Maybe seek therapy—not the Gay bar "Therapy"—a sit-down-and-tell-me-your-problems therapist. God knows it's helped me come to terms with some issues. There is no shame in speaking to someone who can be objective and give you some professional insight.

8. Are you happy?

If your answer to this question is a loud YES! Then move to the next question. If it's a yes with a pause . . . then we may need to figure out when was the last time you were truly happy. It's one of those questions that you cannot lie about even if you want to. Also, it is one of those questions if someone feels the need to ask . . . they may already know the answer.

I want you to think about the last time you were happy. Then think about where you were in your life when you were happy. It is ok if we have to go back to our past to find the answer to this question. Think about how old you were, who you were with, and where you were. Again, a therapist can help a great deal with pointing out these things and shed some light to help you find your way back to happy.

How many of us have looked to other people for *our* happiness? We're all guilty of doing this at some point in time. It's also important to point out that you must be happy with yourself before you can truly be happy with someone else. This is a trait that people can see a mile away, and this attracts people to you. We can tell if someone is putting up a façade of happiness.

We see a lot of this with the "happy" Gay couple. We all know the couple that is putting on a bigger show than the Ringling Brothers. Here's one way of looking at it. Do you know someone who lives check to check, but when you meet up with him he is wearing a high-end pair of shoes. We all know someone like that. We know he can't afford these shoes, but the shoes give the appearance of "I have money!" Meanwhile, he's waiting for you to pay for dinner or buy the next drink. The point is, this person is sending this message that "I'm not broke" to those around him because of a brand he is wearing.

Well, gays do this with relationships; it's almost like people are wearing a brand. As gays, we are smart enough to know what is what when we see it. A lot of the great "brands" can be found on Fifth Avenue, the dysfunctional "brands" come from TJ Maxx, and the fake "brands" come from Canal Street. (Canal Street is in Chinatown, where you can get everything—fake sunglasses, iPhone accessories, Louis Vuitton, even a Mandarin child.) The bottom line is this: You're not fooling anyone by hiding behind your relationship just to appear to be happy. Everyone can see right through it.

This also applies people when they're dating!! Dating someone does not make you appear happier if you're truly not. A friend of mine, who's been single about as long as I have, met someone, and I knew he was falling for this guy. He was flying to visit this guy long distance, bringing him flowers, and spending the week with him when suddenly his attitude changed. At first he was very happy he met a guy he liked and who liked him back. Then he started making comments about me and other friends, telling us we needed to settle down and get what he had. I couldn't believe he was getting cocky because he was dating someone, and some of us weren't. So I thought to myself, *I will give this shit another week, and it will fall apart.* When it did fall apart, you would've thought it was 1929 and the Great Depression started. The relationship fell apart because both parties involved were not in a happy place in their own lives, and one of the two didn't know what he wanted. Now you have honestly answered the questions above for yourself about happiness. Write down your answers, and keep them somewhere private. Go back to whatever you wrote after some time goes by to see where your state of mind was at time. It is a great way to track your personal growth.

Now you may be thinking: *What the hell do I do next?* This requires a lot of what I like to call "me time"—the time I take to myself. Pick any day of the week you have to yourself that's quiet. During this time, I find something from the list of answers to the above questions and attempt to put those issues into some perspective. A glass of wine normally helps with this process (or at least seems sophisticated while dwelling on life). During this "me time," you should dedicate at least one or more uninterrupted hours to yourself. You can also have a whole day that is just for you and your reflections.

> "No problem can be solved until it is reduced to some simple form. The changing of a vague difficulty into a specific, concrete form is a very essential element in thinking."
>
> —J. P. Morgan

Above is one of my favorite quotes. Reflecting takes a lot of work, but I will tell you what works for me. I write down everything, so I encourage you to do the same with your notes for these questions, and rank them by priority, from what is most important to me right now to what is least important. Then, on a new sheet of paper, I want you to elaborate on the one you picked first. When you're done, ask yourself: *How do I fix this?* Say it out loud! Start writing down the thoughts that come to you (and they will). I often find that we know the answers to our own questions if we are honest with ourselves. The Internet is also a great tool for finding information about anything; use it to help resolve or answer some of your questions.

Once you've collected information or found something to point you in the right direction, start making steps to come full circle. Make phone calls to set appointments for everything—doctors, therapists, schools, banks, credit reports, life coaches, your mother—anything you need to get to a stable, comfortable place across the board. Meanwhile, once all of your inner cobwebs are cleaned up, it's time to think about what type of partner will fit your *needs* best.

Have you ever seen a couple walking down the street and said to yourself, "What the hell does he see in that mess?" or "Is that his boyfriend, or is he walking his dog?" or "How did that happen?" Fine, I will admit it: I was the one asking these questions, but in my defense, in most cases, they were valid questions. (Maybe I was still in my Dark Period, a topic I talk about in a later chapter.) Only on the surface did any of those questions matter.

No one knows what goes on behind one's closed doors or what is in one's heart. (Well, almost. We tell our friends just about everything.) But Joe Shmoe on the street doesn't know any information other than what is on the surface or in your Facebook updates.

This brings us to our most important question: What do we want in a partner? This will require some additional "me time" because you really have to be honest about what is truly important to you in a person you'd hope to spend your life—or a long period of time—with. Let's start digging—religion, background, education, vicinity of residence, tall, short, fat, skinny, young, old, ethnic background, etc.

Notice I didn't put anything related to sex here, because we all have our sexual preferences. When you meet the right guy, you'll be surprised how some boundaries are crossed for someone you're in love with. In my opinion, sex becomes a physical manifestation of two people's feelings. We should not put this into the equation right now. For the moment, I do want you think about a Hookup vs. Making Love. The two are very different sexual experiences all together. The feeling of making love to someone can never be replicated with a Hookup. What concerns me is the number of Gay Men who have no idea what I'm talking about. Hopefully, those of you that don't know will meet someone that will help you understand what I am saying.

Back to what we want in a partner, what was listed above is a short list of what could be some deciding factors. If you want a shortcut to all of this, we can take a look at our close friends. Let's be honest: when there isn't anyone special in your life, your friends fill that void to some degree. (There are some itches in life that a close friend just can't scratch.) Still, we choose our friends based on commonalities.

Have you ever heard that old saying, "Birds of a feather flock together"? This is true, for the most part, but people never mention which feather or how many to look for. We all have a group of friends who are all different in their special ways, and you may share something in common with one friend and not the other. This is the same process you'll use when looking for a partner. You'll meet so many different people who may share some of your "feathers" and some who will share none of your feathers. (That's a red flag.) This is where a new list begins; we have to separate ourselves from the superficial things most Gay men look for. Now it's time for a list of what your *needs* are, and please be realistic. Here are a few things on my list:

My Good List (Needs)
1. I need a man who has great communication skills.
2. I need a man who is grounded and compassionate.
3. I need a man who knows what he wants in life.
4. I need a man who is career or goal oriented.
5. It would be nice to have a man who enjoys the arts, but it's not a deal-breaker.
6. Last but not least, he must love dogs! I don't have a dog, but I love them! I know if a dog doesn't like someone, something may be wrong with that person. Just a thought.

Notice I didn't say anything about a big dick or a nice ass, earning six figures, a six-pack stomach, or any other Gay cliché. It's important to separate what you *need* in a partner from the *wants*. There's nothing wrong with having things you want in a partner, but it's about putting our priorities in order.

I used to have a crazy list of things I needed in order to date someone. Then I noticed that my list of requirements was not working out for me. Surprisingly, I found some real men who met these requirements. Again, my list was based on what I *wanted* and not what I *needed*. As a result, I knew that what I really needed was to get my priorities straight.

My Bad List (Wants)
1. Over five foot nine
2. Nice build
3. Straight teeth
4. A career that didn't involve fashion, hair, makeup, etc. (There is nothing wrong with this line of work; I just dated one too many of them.)
5. Earned at least close to six figures
6. Didn't live at home with Mommy
7. Age range from twenty-five to thirty-five

I didn't mention anything in this list that that I genuinely cared about. Everything that is listed above is superficial, but, I still considered myself not as bad as others. I didn't feel like I was looking for America's Next Top Model like some gays. However, I too fell victim to looking for the cliché Gay man. So, I quickly noticed I was picking the wrong type of men for me. Over time I did learn my lesson, and started paying attention to a person's core values. Here are some examples of the things that quickly became my wants and needs, and I want you to do the same thing.

1. *Love?* How important is true love to you?
2. Compatibility—this has many subtopics, but we will go into that in a later chapter.
3. Communication—I can't stress enough how important this is. If two people can't properly communicate with each other, don't even bother moving forward.
4. His heart? You want someone with a compassionate and giving heart, especially if you have one too. If you have a black piece of coal for a heart, then you can just stay single until it is time for you to go to Shady Pines. I genuinely believe that one's ability to be compassionate toward others is one of the things that make someone special.
5. Moral values? If you're a farm boy from the Midwest and you go on a date and find someone with a pentagram on the floor in his apartment, chances are you don't share the same moral values, but if he's cute, you can still kiss him good-night on your way out.

This list can go on and on, but discuss these topics at some point with someone you're getting to know to see where his head is at.

If you haven't picked it up by now, the point of this chapter is to put some things into perspective about life, goals, and growing as an individual. Understanding the importance of knowing what you *need* versus what you *want* in a relationship is crucial. Think about all of the guys you've dated and which ones had some of the qualities you listed above. If you don't know what you want in a man or a relationship, how will you know when it passed you by?

I always say this to people, "If you will waste your time, you will waste mine too." Not knowing what you want or what you're looking for is a waste of precious time. You have to know what you want and how to get it. That applies to everything in life . . . even dating!

Chapter Two

CONFIDENCE

This chapter about confidence will be a bit short, but it is very easy to fix. What I'm going to say may not be easy to hear, but it's important. I'm sure someone has told you that you're beautiful, at some point in your life. Maybe someone has also told you that you're not. It's really easy to let other people convince you of things about yourself; that can mess with your self-esteem.

The reality of confidence is simple: It's not how *others* see you; it's *how you see yourself* that matters. If you look in the mirror and say to yourself, "Oh, hell no!" then maybe you have some work to do. Remember, your appearance should only be about making *you* happy. Fuck what other people think about what you look like! If you're not happy with your appearance, you can't expect anyone else to be.

Living in a city like New York, where real models and actors walk the streets, does not help! (Even though if you've seen some of them in person, you might say, "Damn! Makeup, lights, and smoke work miracles.")

You have to find one thing that makes you special. Some of us have many things that separate us from the masses, but one or two good things are really all you need. Here are some pointers for that:

1. Positive attitude/personality
2. Appearance
3. Profession/special interest
4. Having a brain . . . and using it!

Positive Attitude

If you don't have any friends or no one calls you to see how you're doing, chances are you might have a nasty attitude problem. While I do approve of having a bit of an attitude about *some* things, if it gets to be so bad that you drive people away, that's probably why you're not dating anyone. Fix that right away! There are plenty of books that can help you with that.

If you're an outgoing person with a sense of humor, who smiles a lot and is not afraid to laugh at yourself when you do something stupid, chances are you have a lot of friends, and people want to be around you. Having a great attitude makes you attractive to a possible mate.

Personality

Have you ever seen attractive people and automatically assumed that they must be asswipes or that they are stuck up? Then you manage to speak to them at some point and say to yourself, "Wow, they were really nice." Automatically, this makes them more attractive. This is why personality is so important; it is the biggest moneymaker for attracting people to you. No amount of fitness or white teeth or any physical attribute can take the place of a great personality. If yours sucks, you better get on your knees and say a prayer asking for one. Ultimately, this also ties in with having a positive attitude. Remember, positive energy attracts more positive energy, and having a great personality is one thing that can really make you stand out in a group of people.

Body Types

This is a funny topic. You never know what people are attracted to. You would be surprised to see that guys with some of the hottest bodies will go for the opposite type. So trust me, you don't have to have a bunch of muscles to meet a great guy. Don't assume that a guy with muscles won't want to date you. I will say this: the next time you take a shower, go stand in front of a mirror and drop the towel. Now if you say to yourself, "Damn, I'm a sexy bitch" (I say that now), then you're good to go. If you drop your towel and say, "Oh, hell no" (I used to say that too), then you need to fix it. If you drop your towel and say to yourself, "Hmm . . . there are some areas in question, but I'm still cute" (I used to say that too), then you're probably in a good place with your confidence level. The bottom line again is this: If you're not happy with your body, how do you want someone else to be happy with it? There is a good chance this will affect your confidence as well.

Face

Now this one is a doozey. The face is the first thing people see when they look at you. Studies have shown that humans look for genetic markers when looking for a mate. What do the gays do? They scan you from head to toe. If you have matured and outgrown that phase, you will look a bit deeper than a symmetrical face. I think we have all fallen for a pretty face at one time or another. I remember one of my exes was everything I thought I wanted in a boyfriend. Physically, he looked exactly like I wanted my boyfriend to look, but when I tried to have a conversation with him it was like he needed help just to think. The answer I would get for everything was, "I don't know."

Finally, one day after many questions, I said, "Motherfucker, what *do* you know?" Well, I'm sure you can see *that* didn't work out. So back to the face issue . . . everyone (hopefully) has one facial feature that will be seen as attractive to someone. If you're not the town beauty, then you have to stick to the basics. We all have skin, teeth, hair. (If you only have two out of three, it's okay, boo. Just keep everything clean!) I mean, really, if you're older than your mid-twenties and you have acne, go see a dermatologist. If your teeth look like a toolbox, go see an orthodontist. Or at least go get them whitened professionally and cleaned by a dentist twice a year. As for your hair, just keep it nice and neat. It seems simple, right? It's not as hard as trying to figure out why people care about the Kardashians. (Yeah, I don't get it either.) I can tell you firsthand about all of the corn teeth and rat's-nest heads and pepperoni faces I see walking around Manhattan. There is no reason to be careless about any of this, and you send a message to other people that you may not care about yourself, and that can be an unattractive trait.

Height

Most of the times when you hear people describe what kind of guy they want in their life, the first thing they say is "I want someone tall!" Well, not everyone is over six feet.

If you were born in the 1980s in this country, you may have watched the Smurfs. If you're like Gargamel and like chasing around little men with funny shoes, you're in the right place. I was not surprised when they made the Smurfs movie based out of NYC. You will not have any problem finding a smart, cute, short guy in New York City. So if you're short, don't worry. There will always be someone who wants to pin you down. If you're like me, a tall man who likes other tall men, things can become a bit harder. Try to find a middle ground that you can deal with. Remember, this should never be an issue with your confidence. There is always someone out there who will fit the bill.

Profession

Discussing topic number three, profession or careers, is easy because most people are proud to discuss what they do for a living if it is interesting. If your job is along the lines of cleaning the lint out of the dryers at the Laundromat (and if you're happy with that), then we may need to reconsider some priorities, and dating is not one of them.

If you're not happy to wake up and go to your job every day, then you need another job! It's important to do something you love to do, even if you don't make a lot of money at first. It's okay. If you *love* what you do, then the money tends to come later. This applies to someone you're dating too. If someone has the potential to be successful, don't just dismiss him. You never know if, a year or two later, he will be in a different position, making a lot of money, but won't date you now because he knows that's all you care about. Ultimately, it does not really matter to most people what you do for a living, but being passionate about your career or goals is a very attractive trait!

Special Interests

Learning about the little things that people are interested in is always interesting. Now, I'm a big guy—six foot two, 230, with a muscular frame. A lot of people look at me and assume that I'm only into gym-related things. That's far from the truth. I'm just a nerd who's always been active but still a nerd. I've collected coins and stamps since I was a kid. I love baseball, theater, dance performances, and the opera. I also love foreign films and period pieces and British literature. In addition to being an avid watcher of the stock market, I enjoy following financial news. Those are many of my special interests, but you wouldn't know it by looking at me.

All of these details tell you much more about a person and are not normally revealed until after you've known a person for a while. I find that if you convey your special interests first, this opens the door for someone you're seeing to do the same. Think about the connection that could be created if two people are attracted to each other and share some of the same interests. This could spark all kinds of things.

Having a Brain . . . and Using It!

This one is may sound funny, but make sure the guy you're dating doesn't have to share a brain with someone else to give you one complete thought. I love a smart man! It's the biggest turn-on for me. Most smart people have great communication skills, and we know that communication is very important between two people. If the person you're dating asks you, "Who is your favorite Kardashian?" (And if you have an answer, that's even more disturbing), and this is the nature of your discussions, you may be wondering: *What the hell I am I doing with this person?* Just put that person into the "friend box," or if he's really, really, *really* sexy, put him in the "dick in a glass" category, but don't be rude.

It's important to look for someone with the same mental capability as you or at least close to it. I mean, after the sex is over, what else is left? Exactly! I have been there too.

If you're not the sharpest tool in the box, it's okay; just try to stay on top of the latest local and global current events. Besides, there are a lot of people out there pretending to be smart and getting away with it.

You may have heard the phrase, "confidence is key." I completely agree with this, and I'm not going to re-invent the wheel on this one. Let me just say that self-confidence is the key that opens every door you want to open. It may take some time to develop this if you have a problem feeling as confident as you should, but keep reviewing the topics above. I'm sure you will get the hang of it. Also, being confident will always help you meet new and interesting men to date.

Chapter Three

PUTTING YOURSELF OUT THERE

"Putting yourself out there"—I hate this common saying, because it is such a clichéd thing to say to someone who is single. It's almost like someone giving you dating advice . . . oh, wait a minute, I'm doing that too. It's normally from one of your friends who is in an open . . . oops, I mean long-term relationship. Even worse, you might hear this from a friend of yours who's just met someone. (Just wait a few weeks; you can throw this back in his face.)

Please feel free to stand up and smack him if one of them says this to you (or find something about him to make a shady comment on). In a way, it is a kind of pity phrase to say to someone; you might as well say, "You're not really that attractive, and you should lower your standards."

In their defense, I'm sure this comes from a good place when someone says this nasty phrase. We know he cares about us, and he's just trying to help, but it's just something you don't need to be reminded of. Most people feel like if you're single, life must be hard, or they will try to set you up with someone. There must be something to saying this phrase, because we hear it everywhere.

Let's take a minute and think to ourselves about what this really means. My interpretation of this phase mostly involves keeping an open mind to what is around you. When you live in a city like New York or any big city, it is easy have your guard up about a lot of things: keys, wallets, smartphones, crazy ex-boyfriends, and late train or bus rides. We can be guarded with who we are in public as well. I want you to let the guard down just a little bit; it will pay off. For example, I think a simple smile to a stranger and just being polite to someone are things other people may see. We never know if there is an interested guy watching us, and these kind gestures send a positive message about ourselves to someone we don't even know is watching.

Try this: put on something nice, and make a few plans. Go meet a friend for Sunday brunch in a non-gayborhood and sit in the middle of the restaurant (or at least somewhere you can have the best view of who is in the place). Have a great conversation about current events, work, family, or some advice you may have given. (This works well if the friend is not gay, and it helps if he or she is smart. It works with either a guy or a girl.) If you causally mention you're gay, watch how many ears perk up—but keep it cool. This alone puts so much about who you are as a person out there; it's crazy. You will seem like a confident, interesting person someone would want to come say hello to.

Now in case you're wondering what the hell this has to do with anything, let's think about it for a second. How many times are we on the train, and we see some of the same people around the same time of day? How many times do you see the same people at the gym the same times you're working out? I think you get the picture. When you're always being your real self, you seem approachable. That's our goal of "putting ourselves out there"—being more approachable. Having a nice face and great body will not necessarily help with this; actually those guys have it really hard, but we will talk about that in a later chapter. People want to be around, speak to, and associate with people they can relate to.

Now, the cliché "Putting yourself out there" for me really just means being open to all avenues of meeting someone, online dating, clubs, bars blah blah. We now know that this is not how we will use this evil phrase. Moving forward we are going to change the meaning of "putting yourself out there" into "making ourselves approachable." Being approachable in public will get you more dates.

Have you ever gotten dressed and gone to a bar, and absolutely no one said one word to you? Yeah, I know . . . sad. Let's think about what you were doing that night. Were you in a shady corner? Were your arms folded? Did you look like you were having a good time even though you were alone? If your answers to the first two questions were *yes* and the third *no,* you may have sent the wrong message out to people.

What about your online profile? Do you have one of those "bitter" profiles, listing all of the things you *don't* want in a person? Again, this sends out a negative message.

So what point am I trying to make? If you ever watched *The Nanny,* you know she wore too much makeup and short skirts and big hair. Her character screamed *I'm available!* That's what I want you to do too . . . well, not everything, but whatever message you want people to get needs to be clear.

"Hello, I am single, sexy, happy, and mentally sane. Come talk to me!" That's the message I want to see you have, out at a bar or club, even online.

Chapter Four

BARS, CLUBS, AND LOUNGES, OH MY!

There's no place like home, there's no place like home . . . my ass!

Sometimes when you go to a Gay establishment, you feel like you're on the damn yellow brick road. It seems like you're going from one bar to another and another, and instead of finding the Wicked Witch of the West, you see Bianca Del Rio. (I love her—she is an NYC drag queen who is funny as hell!) Then you think different people will be at this bar, but all of the people start to look the same. Then you realize these bitches are doing the same thing you're doing, because you just saw them. The gays are going from one bar to another, just like you, and then the yellow brick road turns into a fucking Gay pride parade.

We always ask ourselves this question when we decide to go out: Do we go out alone or with friends? Both options have their benefits. Hanging out with friends gives us a sense of security in a public setting. Sometimes we need a wingman to help give us the courage to walk up to a guy we think is cute.

Sidebar: Why does a Gay bar remind us of the high school lunchroom? You've got the skinny bitches, jocks, wannabe jocks, nerds, weird goths, punk/Sharon Needles types . . . pretty girls, pretty boys. Yes, I've seen the movie *Mean Girls* several times, but that's a cute version of American high schools. These kids are brutal! And what's worse, the same activity can take place among grown-ass Gay men.

. . . and we're back! Yes, our friends and a few cocktails give us a bit of motivation to walk up to guy, but then what do you say? We'll come back to that in a moment. Now let's talk about what typically happens when you go out alone. This one is my personal favorite. When you go out alone, you kind of place yourself into one of two categories. You're either the creepy, freaky Gay or the mysterious gay. Both have their purposes. I'm not saying this is okay, but let's be honest: A lot of times, guys go out alone so they can leave with someone else. We all know the creepy guy when we see him, because he looks like a dog that just did a trick and is waiting for his treat.

Then you have the mysterious Gay guy. If you've ever seen a fashion show, all the models have a bored look on their faces, but they look great, and you're kind of drawn to them, but you don't know why. Well, that's part of the mysterious gay, but you're going to be a bit more pleasant than that. You'll walk in with that bored but confident look on your face. If you see someone noticing you when you first walk in, you smile and acknowledge him, but your destination is the bar and getting your first drink. If you don't drink alcohol, get cranberry juice or seltzer water—just get *something.* No one wants to be that guy at a bar who just stands around and says, "I don't drink." Really? I mean, why are you there?

Now that you have your drink, if there is space at the bar, stay there. It's a focal point, and it ensures you're seen by almost everyone. If there isn't any space at the bar, go somewhere not too far from the bar, but with enough distance from other people so it's clear you're not part of a group. Now just stand there. I know what you're thinking: *All of this drama just to stand there?* Well, it gets better; you're going to seem a bit odd at first. You're alone, having your drink. If there's a song playing that you like, bob your head a little. This sends a message out that you're confident and don't need a clique to enjoy yourself. If you do it well, you'll be surprised how a guy or several guys start walking up to you to introduce themselves.

Now that you have gotten someone's attention, keep things cool. Shake his hand (like a man, even if you are a fairy); always keep eye contact when you're talking to him, and if you're interested, keep talking to him. Don't start asking questions like you're conducting an interview;

people hate this. Compliment him on something. It can be anything; just be creative.

Here comes a bit of a hard part at a bar or a club. What do you do when you're talking to someone you like and a friend walks up? We know that the Gay community is very small, no matter how big the city; we will always run into someone somewhere. This new person you just met is going to watch you like he is on a keto diet, and you're a big slice of pizza. (Don't you hate that? You're on a diet, and everything you see reminds you of food.) This pizza he is watching already has all of the toppings he wants, but he is going to look for one thing he *doesn't* want on his slice. I say all that to say this: Your body language with this friend of yours will speak louder than all of the speakers in the place.

So defuse the situation; make sure you greet your friend the way you normally would, and then introduce your new friend. Give the hint that you're trying to talk to him, and try to get rid of this friend. When the friend goes away, give a brief description of who he or she is, and move on to the next subject. If this guy is still there with you, offer to buy him a drink, and see where it goes. If you see that the interest is mutual, exchange numbers.

During this whole time, someone else who may be interested in you just sits back and watches this whole scenario play out. Depending how well you did with the first guy, others will get the nerve to come talk to you.

Just repeat the same thing, but remember, you don't want to give off the vibe that you're there with someone. With each person you speak to, you become more and more approachable, and that's our goal.

We left out one key player in this: The guy who didn't have the nerve, and when he did, you were talking to someone else. He will wait until he sees you again, but this time, it will be anywhere—the street, the subway, Grindr, Jack'd, Facebook. Remember to be polite; you may not remember where he saw you, but if you're interested, it's your chance to make a *great* first impression. These rules apply just about anywhere, in any environment; just give it a try, and see what happens.

Chapter Five

ONLINE DATING

This next chapter is messier than the West Village after Gay Pride, Halloween, or any weekend, but it's a topic that needs to be discussed. There are so many things to look out for online. You have a lot of terms you have to learn with online dating profiles, such as PNP, BB, partying, pros, smack, anything goes (not the Broadway play); the list of online code words goes on and on. God forbid you're newly single and don't know what a lot of these terms even mean. You will be like a lamb surrounded by a large pack of Gay wolves.

You can look at online dating a few different ways, depending on how old you are. Let's talk about online dating for my age group, late twenties to mid-thirties. We grew up in the '80s, when HIV and AIDS were in the newspapers and talk shows every day, and people were saying that the gays were the cause of this disease. Imagine being a young boy, knowing you liked other boys, and hearing that older men like you were beaten up and killed just for being gay. This creates a need to be more self-aware of your mannerisms and how you carried yourself. The need to be masculine follows you into your adulthood, and for the most part it affects a lot of the ways you interact with others and how others perceive you. How does this affect online dating? We will get to that in a bit.

What about the older gays? I mean, let's be honest—online dating wasn't really around prior to 1995. This is where interpersonal skills got you a date, sex, friends, or whatever. Have you noticed it's easier to speak to an older Gay man, and they seem to know just what to say to you? Being friendly and polite went a long way with the gays prior to the Internet. A Gay bar or club was a necessity for meeting people, because online options were not available.

I personally feel that this age group of Gay men had the most fun. If you wanted to meet someone, you had no choice but to go out. Instead of having profiles on different hookup websites and apps, they had to meet in known Gay hangouts. So I find that online dating for that age group is easier in terms of communicating, mostly because they know how to be polite and respect other people.

I find that most of the bitter profiles tend to be from the gays in my age group. Since the need to be or appear "masculine" seems to be a huge issue with guys, it's important for them to have this masculine-sounding profile with masculine-looking pictures. Then you meet most of them, and they are gayer than Fifth Avenue on Gay Pride weekend. So many of them are pretending to be one way rather than another; guys are often disappointed once they meet or talk to the pretender in person. Then comes the bitterness. For me, the bitterness comes from people expecting something other than a person being genuine and kind.

Often you will find profiles where guys talk about what they *don't* like, and they never seem to match their own requests. Avoid these people like the plague—or anyone with any negative thing to say on their profile. Remember, this is a representation of who you are, so don't waste any words or time on anyone who's negative.

We now come to the "baby gays" and online dating. These little bitches were born around the early to mid-1990s. Talk about aggressive, pushy, and straight to the point! At twenty-three, I was even scared to say the word *gay*. These next-gen gays are off the chain! I wonder at times, do you even know how much fighting, marching, bloodshed, and lost lives had taken place so you can be a little freer to be yourselves?

You have to respect that a lot of the "up-and-coming children" are a little more developed when it comes to what they want. I believe this is due to the younger gays experiencing life and accepting themselves as being Gay at a much earlier age than a lot of us older gays did. A lot of them had their first boyfriend at fifteen and feel that they are ready for something serious. Really, who wants to babysit? I have to admit, a lot of them are so cute, and it's hard to resist some of them.

Now for the dark part of online dating. Yes, I have to go here. It's not a pleasant subject, but it's important. Drugs, raw sex, sex parties, meth, HIV, herpes, hepatitis, open relationships, Partying and Playing . . . . R U Looking? (I hate people who use "R U looking" as a form of initial communication. I mean, really! I want to look to punch you in the face.) These are all huge red flags. I find that large populations of the Gay community are participating in a lot of crazy, careless, self-destructive activities related to drugs and sex. A lot of these things are related to a person going through a <u>Dark Period</u>; I talk more about that in a later chapter. You would think it was the 1970s, when people carried on like life was live porno. I'm not going to lie; I'm sure being carefree feels good, but it all has its causes and effects. I understand we're all adults, and everyone has the right to do what he wants. What happens when you go to a Gay website? Initially the websites were mainly geared toward single Gay men for dating and hooking up. Then you started to see dating sites filled with "other" profiles. You can see as many partners, or open-relationship, sex-party profiles, and prostitutes mixed in with regular, single Gay guys. These things can make online dating very frustrating, but I still feel it's a necessary evil.

There are a lot of websites and Gay applications for phones out there—Adam4Adam.com, Manhunt.com, Realjock.com, Grindr, Jack'd, just to name some of the popular ones. If I had to pick a dating app, I would go with Jack'd over Grindr, simply because a lot of Grindr profiles appear to only be about looking for sex. Jack'd allows you to express more of yourself and gives you more insight into a person. Jack'd also allows you to put more than one picture on your profile. Remember, we want to send the right message to people.

The websites are a bit tricky; it's important to read the profiles you're interested in so you can weed out the messy men you don't want. Another thing you will find in reading profiles closely is that you will get a sense of what kind of guy you're talking to. Engage him a bit online, and if he seems cool, then exchange numbers and see if the conversation is still pleasant. If someone cannot be cordial online, chances are he won't be cordial in person. For example, if you give a compliment to someone's profile like, "Hi, I like your profile," and they reply with "Open pics," this is not someone you want to meet.

There is never an excuse for rude behavior—ever! My personal pet peeve is when someone greets you with "R U Looking?" I'm always shocked; who does that? Maybe I'm a bit old-fashioned, but a nice, "Hello, how are you?" will go a long way with most people. If you're that desperate and high and horny that you can't even address someone properly, again this is always trouble. A lot of those "Looking" guys are looking for another hot mess to be messy with. Don't even reply to these guys, and if anything, block them right away.

I find that you will always encounter two types of people; either you're a sheep, or you're a shepherd. In some cases, you want to be the black sheep. The sheep just follow whatever the other sheep are doing, no matter how stupid it is. I think we have a lot of Gay sheep who would follow other sheep into an oven if they thought it was where everyone else was going. The shepherd and the occasional black sheep are a leader and more of a free thinker. He doesn't need anyone to tell him what is cool or hot and what he should be doing because he's gay. He can stand up for what he wants and does not let the pressure of the community or anyone dictate what and how he should be.

If one sheep goes and gets high, the other sheep will follow him into the bathroom to do it too. If another sheep goes and gets a butt implant, someone else will go and do that. Even if a sheep sees another sheep overdose at a party, it won't stop him from using the same drug over and over. If a sheep says, "I want to get muscles. Let me do steroids, but I heard a few people died as a result of this," we know another sheep will go and do it too.

I guess by now you see where I'm going with this. It's a hot, homeless-on-the-subway, sweaty, smelly mess. We have to clean up our act! We fight for equal rights and complain when someone says something bad about the Gay community. Well, there, I said it.

Now that I'm off my soapbox, I'll say that online dating is just like I described. You have people doing the same thing they see other people doing. You can tell by the headless torso pics that you'll find on most online profiles. With all of that said, please use your best judgment when trying online dating. It's a great tool to meet a lot of great guys, but sometimes the bad outweighs the good.

Everyone has different opinions on how to go about online dating. My opinion is that if you look for something, you will find it. If you're looking for a hookup, you'll find it. If you're looking for someone to have a nice conversation with, you'll find it. If you're looking for someone who can meet you for a date, you'll find it as well. You just have to keep an open mind and know what you will and won't put up with.

So remember, online dating can be really easy. Just take one or two nice pics. (Don't get into this thing where people are putting whole photo shoots online. Really?) Your profile pic is important, but think about how many people you've met in person whose pic was not exactly accurate. We all have different views of what we see; like people say, "Beauty is in the eye of the beholder."

An online picture can't compete with a face-to-face meeting, so don't put too much into this. Guess what: Those guys who want you to send them a full book of pictures? Avoid them too. They normally have issues anyway. (And am I the only one who thinks that the ones who have a list of what you should look like never look like anything in the first place?)

So, when you are writing your profile details think about the type of guys you want to read them and send you a message. Remember, don't write about what you do not want; say what you do want. Mark sure to include some of the things that make you interesting. Mention any hobbies, fitness, theater, music, movies—any activities that can make you relatable to other guys. You want someone that likes your profile to say, "Hi, I enjoy that too." If you approach online dating with positive thinking, then you should have a positive outcome.

Chapter Six

SEX, SEX, AND MORE SEX

Sex, sex, sex . . . . I know, I know, we all love it, and some of us can't get enough of it, but a hyper sexual lifestyle is the perception that people outside of the Gay community have of us. I would not say that it's completely false, but a lot of guys including myself can't just jump into bed with someone unless I feel something for them. I do believe that as adults, it's important for us to have an open discussion about sex. It seems that Americans have more social and mental hang-ups about sex than any other modern culture. I feel our puritan-based ideologies are the real reason that half of the general public has a problem with the Gay Community. It appears to me it's not the fact of being gay; it's the sexual act of it that bothers most straight people.

I look at it like this: what goes on behind closed doors is no one's business but your own. Gay or straight, it still applies. How you decide to carry yourself outside of that private setting is up to you.

Therefore, sex needs to be discussed with someone you're thinking about dating—preferably *after* you've gotten to know the Man you're dating a bit. Now let's paint a picture: You meet a guy online or at a bar or club. Then you spend a few days talking on the phone getting better acquainted with this person. One person wants to see when you're available to meet up, and the first date is set.

Now, that's all fine and dandy, but the topic of sex may or may not have been discussed. Let's be honest—I don't believe that asking someone if they're a "top" or a "bottom" within the first five minutes of talking is appropriate. Especially if your goal is it date a nice guy, not hooking up. (That question is asked every day, and yes, this is a red flag! Run away.) Another thing that annoys me is this question: "How big is your dick?" (A greedy bottom normally asks this question.) Really? Again, red flag. Run *far away.* Nonetheless, sex is a topic that should be talked about at the appropriate time like two smart adults.

However, we are talking about two *men,* and we are testosterone-driven creatures. We are not monkeys, though; we are sophisticated adults that can control our actions. Straight men wouldn't dare speak to a woman they are interested in about sex until a much longer period of time has gone by, but straight people don't really have to worry about what role one has to play in bed, do they?

So this is the only valid reason Gay Men would need to have this discussion to see if both people are compatible.

How do you start this conversation? One way would be to compliment this person on a physical attribute of his body. We all have things we like about a man; just pick one you like, and flatter him. Do not be afraid to give compliments; it will not cost you anything; it's free. (Sidebar: Flattery is the key to getting a lot of what you want. It works, but it needs to be sincere and not creepy.) Another way would be to tell a story about one of your past sexual encounters and talk about what you liked and didn't like. Allow him to reply to you and share one of his stories, and just go back and forth. At some point, the questions will become more and more probing. (Talking like this could get both parties hotter than a Gay farm boy's first time in NYC. It can also be just as scary.) So make sure you pay close attention to each other's responses or lack of responses. It's also important not to be judgmental, no matter what the other person says. (Unless he wants to pee on you . . . . Kidding.)

Talking about sex creates a perfect opportunity to ask a simple but important question: "Are you HIV-positive?" This question will either be answered quickly with a *yes* or *no* or with hesitation or some off-the-wall answer. Pay close attention to the guy's answer to this question. I sometimes ask this question in person, to get a face-to-face reaction. The body language of a person after this question will tell you a lot. I'm HIV-negative, but I still make a point to get tested twice a year, every June and January.

I have dated a few guys who were HIV-positive, and when they told me, I didn't treat them any differently. I actually respected them for being up-front and honest with me about it. There are so many Gay men who know they are positive and lie about it to their sexual partners. It is more likely that someone will not disclose this information when you're meeting for a hookup. If you have gotten to know someone for a while before having sex with him, he is more likely to tell you on his own if he is positive. Also, for the record, guys: lying about your HIV status is against the law. It's called the HIV Reporting/Partner Notification Law in the state of New York. Thirty-two states have this law listed on their websites; please read it. It's not one-sided; if you are HIV-positive, it also protects you from any discrimination. For me, what is more dangerous are the people who don't know they are positive and just carry on like nothing is going on in their life. The men who told me about their status, I would always ask about their viral load, white blood cell count, and if they were undetectable or not, and then keep it moving. I often find that a lot of HIV-positive men have insecurities and coping issues related to this, and that alone could make dating them a problem. I would recommend if you are HIV-positive and have not come to terms with it, please go see a counselor so you can privately discuss your concerns and move on in your life. There are worse things that can happen to you in life besides catching this virus.

By now we have made a decision—whether we know it or not—but we have subconsciously decided how we will move forward with this person sexually. Unless you're the type of guy who has very strict rules about what you're into sexually, and you're not open to possibilities; then you might want to date someone who also feels the same way about sexual roles and where they fit into all of that. If you're open about sex and flexible about what can happen, if you have dated someone for a while and developed feelings, you may be open to other things that may not be your preference. I personally believe that when you're open regarding sexual roles, your number of potential mates is higher.

Me personally, I like to date a guy that I don't know right away what role he plays in bed. We all know that our brain is the most important sex organ. Not knowing what role he plays allows me to fantasize about him every night, what I want to do to him, and what I might let him do to me. Then passion and emotions with a side of lust is mixed in and builds up the longer you wait while you're getting to know the person. You have put so much thought into what you're going to do sexually, and when it finally happens it's like the 4th of July.

Let's really look closer into the benefits of not rushing into sex while dating. Things like, a simple touch of his legs or holding hands can turn you on. So we need to stop rushing to the nearest bed and rush to get the nerve to just hold his hand. Imagine that!! (Remember we are not in a "DP" if we are dating . . . . and bed hopping is a sign of a "DP") Then the next move would be getting to the first kiss!! Now this is one of my favorite things to do!! I love kissing, and everyone does it differently. Picture someone you are dating, and fantasize about him kissing you for the first time. WHOA!! The first kiss changes everything, because now you're no longer wondering what it feels like; now you know. Then you take your thoughts and fantasy other places because you have something to base it on. I think you're getting the picture; allow your brain to process all of these things. If he is really worth dating, he is worth waiting until the time is right to have sex. Stimulate your mind with the thoughts of the man you are dating. This will help in building a stronger connection to a person that may lead to a long-term serious relationship that is not based on sex.

What if the man you are dating does not want to wait? Oh well!! Keep it moving!! In his eyes you should be worth the wait until you're ready. However, all men have egos, and Gay men seem to have bigger egos than normal. (Easily fragile egos is more like it.) It's like a little brat with a lot of toys. The little brat didn't want the toy until another little kid wanted to play with it. What makes this feeling even worse is when it is a toy the damn kid didn't play with yet. The kid will do just about anything to get that toy in his hand, but when the toy is gone, and the other kid takes it home, it's too late. Poor little Pablo will dream, thinking about that toy for a while.

Try it and see what happens; this alone will also give you a little more confidence—just to let the man you're dating see you are not the average Gay guy out there and there is more to you than just sex. Remember sex is very easy to find, but getting to know someone takes an effort; it's a two way street, and you want a person to meet you half way.

This topic of sex would not be complete unless I did my duty and discussed safe sex, or more to the point, the *lack* of safe sex that seems to have become popular again like it's the '70s. I believe a lot of it is due to the large amount of unprotected sex or raw Gay porn that's grown in popularity. Yes, I know it's hot, and I watch a lot of it myself, but it's important to remember the difference between something you're watching and real life. The other reason I believe unsafe sex has become more prevalent is the large number of Gay men who are HIV-positive. A friend told me that the new thing in the city is that gays would hook up, and if neither party mentions the use of a condom, it's automatically assumed that both guys are positive, and no questions are asked.

Really, people? Come on; we all know better than this, but again, this is the self-destructive behavior that is becoming more common with a lot of Gay men. I took the advice of another old friend of mine. He says, "Treat everyone as if . . . ." meaning have safe sex, no matter what someone tells you.

I have been in a few situations where I was with a guy, and things were hot and heavy, and we could have easily just done everything without a condom. There is always a moment to think before you go too far! Make sure you *stop* and grab a condom. For you bottoms out there, don't just assume the guy has put a condom on; reach behind you, and feel for it before he puts it in you each time.

The Gay community in any city anywhere is very small. It never fails; we always run into each other at some point—ex-boyfriends, people you dated, guys you hooked up with. (Some of you cannot even remember names or faces.) It's always important to be respectful of these "lovers." You never know who knows who in the Gay community. I want you to remember to be respectful to everyone. The last guy you hooked up with or dated could easily be best friends with someone new you met who you think is "the one." Just keep that in mind at all times; you don't want this biting you in the ass later.

Chapter Seven

FIRST DATE

I'm finding that a lot of Gay guys don't know what the phrase "a date" means. I mean that in the traditional ("straight") sense of the term—a man will ask out a woman he's interested in. She pretends to be coy and say cute little things like, "Let me check my calendar"; then she gives a day or time she's free. He picks and plans the date . . . and pays for the date. (I know a lot of women want to be treated like equals on so many levels, but dating is the one time they still expect to be treated like a lady.) Well, in the Gay community, a date means something different to everybody. Most Gay dates range from a hookup to a meeting at Starbucks. I know dating is really an area that Gay men need to work on. First things first: I want to say that hooking up is not a date. It's a booty call! A date, according to *Webster's Dictionary,* is an appointment to meet for a social engagement. It has a romantic nature to it.

Dating is one of my favorite things to talk about. You may be surprised to learn that a lot of guys have never been on a *real* date. Hell, there are a lot of guys who have never even been to a concert, a play, Central Park, etc. A lot of guys are just used to the idea that a date equals a hookup. So what's so different with Gay dating as opposed to straight dating? Well, we can't play the role of the women we see on TV when it comes to being asked out. Remember, it's *two men!* So it should be as simple as this: "Hey, I got Yankees tickets. Do you want to go?" Yes, I know . . . it's really that easy. The traditional rules of dating don't apply to the gays, at least not yet. What I'm trying to say is that a random Gay man normally wouldn't walk up to another Gay guy and say, "Hi, can I buy you a drink?" Yeah, I know, this does happen from time to time, but I would not say this is normal in a setting that is not gay.

A lot of us need to go through so much to meet people. Then again, there is "the eye." This is a look two Gay men give each other in a public setting that is not gay. One person stops and sees if the other guy looks back, and then one person walks back. Yes, that happens a lot, and sometimes you find out he's a hustler looking for a dollar and a date. So we have to go through the meeting at a bar or club, online, apps, long-ass phone calls, and then a first date is set. "So you want to come over? We can hang out and watch a movie."

Okay, boys and boy-girls, this could be a tricky one. I've done this for a first date before, but normally it is a hookup disguised as a date.

If this happens make sure you're being clear that you're looking to get to know someone better and not quickly jump into bed. If you are meeting someone for the first time, never go to his place! That is a booty call. My mother used to say, "Nothing is open past 2:00 a.m. but some legs." (This was in the '80s in the Midwest.)

Now, *this* is a proper way to ask for a date: "Well, I have really enjoyed talking to you these past few days. I would like for us to go out so we can talk more. Would you like to meet somewhere for dinner or a drink?" Gay or straight, this is how you ask someone to spend time with you. The only difference is when and where the date is asked, but your response should be along these lines.

"Yes, I would like that a lot. Let's agree on a time and place, and I will see you there." That is a proper response to a date request. (Yes, I know I'm not talking to kids, but a lot of gays don't know why people don't react to them after a date has been offered. The response needs to be *genuine.*) So what just happened above involved two people, with one offering to take the other, someone he is getting acquainted with to the next level. Before a full-blown date is set up, do something kind of light; just meet for a drink or coffee or a walk to Central Park. (For those of you not in New York City, just go to any city park and enjoy yourself.) This needs to be done to see if there is genuine chemistry between the two of you. There's no need to waste time or money if it's clear that it's not going to work out. Let's face it; some people are shady bitches. There can be one thing wrong with a guy, and you're ready to drop-kick him to the sewer. So what if his teeth look like tools in a drawer? (I'm not going to lie—that happened to me, and I had to think about kissing him and worrying if he would give me gingivitis.) If you meet a guy and you are not interested in anything more then being friends, just be a man about it and tell him.

Hopefully the meet-and-greet goes well, the attraction is there, and the conversations are the same in person as on the phone. Don't you hate when someone is engaging on the phone, but then, when you meet him, he only gives you one-word answers. So anyway, if you think the chemistry is great and things are flowing, then everything is good. Cut it short. Now the interest is mutual; it's time to set the first date.

Now, boys and boy-girls, it's time for the fun part—the actual date! This should be an exciting thing to do. There is a lot of tension already built up from the meet-and-greet. So now we have a few things to do to prepare for this date. Let's think about past conversations you've had with this guy. If he mentioned anything that the two of you have in common—food, sights in the city, theater—that should be part of the first date. Add in something new that the two of you never mentioned but you think would be nice to do.

Try to write down any ideas you may have for the date, if you're the one planning. Make sure you think about the weather and things like dress codes of certain restaurants. This leads you to what you're going to wear, haircuts, shoes . . . and wear nice underwear, please! (There is no bigger turnoff than holes in someone's underwear.)

Just in case you go back to your place for a glass of wine, make sure your place is presentable. (If you don't have wine, go get some!) Lay out everything you need before the date; this way, if it's during the week, you're not rushing home after work to pull things together at the last minute. Also, be early—but not too early; no one wants his time wasted, and just in case your hair is not dry yet, you can check it before he shows up. Oh, I almost forgot: please watch the news the day before, so you won't look crazy if the topic of local news comes up. It doesn't matter as much if you know any world news, but you should at least know what the hell is going on in your city or neighborhood. Checked off everything on your list? Good, now you're ready . . . well, almost.

It's important on the first date to move slowly, for multiple reasons. First, you cannot let your imagination get the best of you. From time to time, we start to fast-forward and imagine what it would be like if we were in a relationship with this person. We dream about the possibilities. *Stop* that shit now! If we let our imagination get the best of us, all it leads to is a possible huge disappointment if it doesn't work out. So take it one damn day at a time; just let things flow, and just be open with how you feel.

Now here is a bit from my dating experiences in New York City. I kept doing things the wrong way. When I became single, I was expecting my Gay fairytale to happen for me all over again. Instead I kept running into Gay nightmares. I was meeting guys and talking to them for a bit. Then, at our first meeting, I went all out: nice dinner or a Broadway show or a walk to Central Park. I was doing things that I thought were nice for a first date. I quickly learned that a lot of guys never had this kind of treatment, or if they were lucky and they might have gone to a movie with a guy, they were clearly not the kind of dates I was planning. Not to mention that the cost of this shit started to add up, because things didn't work out a lot of times. Maybe I can write a letter to President Obama to say, "If you're going to tax single people at a higher federal tax rate, we should be able to write off our dating expenses." Just a thought.

I was complaining to a friend about it, and he told me I was doing too much too soon. He was telling me to keep it simple for the first time you meet. So I took his advice, and this worked out a lot better for me and my

American Express card. You will know right away if you click with someone over a cup of coffee or a nice gin and tonic (my favorite drink), more than you would over an expensive dinner or theater tickets. Besides, it makes meeting someone for the first time more comfortable in a laid-back setting. Hell, the first date is nerve-wracking as it is.

Then it dawned on me that I wasn't really doing a bad thing by taking these guys out the way I wanted. I was not doing anything wrong. I kept meeting these emotionally damaged Gay guys with a lot of bad past experiences. When a guy comes along and takes them out on a *real* date, they don't know how to act. Sometimes people get so used to guys treating them like the lint in the dryer, they expect that when they meet people. So a nice guy shows up, and they're so happy that someone treated them nicely, and they think they've fallen in love, when it's only the first damn date. Trust me, it happens to me. (Just so we're clear, I wasn't the one falling in love; I was the one who took someone out on a date, and he turned into . . . what? A stalker! He was cute, so I didn't mind as much.) Or the worst happens: the guy is freaked out because someone treated him with some respect and showed him a good time that didn't involve a bedroom, and he runs away. I hate that. If you're not emotionally, physically, or financially ready to get to know someone, you should be honest with yourself and the other person right away. If you know you're not ready to date people, stay out of that market and work on yourself until you *are* ready.

We've come a long way, haven't we? We've talked about deciding what we want from a relationship or a person we're interested in dating. Also, at this point, we've had several conversations on the phone; we are texting each other throughout the day. By now, you should have established a pretty good idea of the type of guy you're dealing with. A proper date has been set up, and everything is ready to go. Have fun, and remember: The purpose of this date is to get to know this person better.

Oh yes, I almost forgot one more thing: sex on a first date. The old-fashioned part of me screams "hell no," but then the slutty part of me says "maybe." If it's "maybe," make sure condoms and your favorite lube and "other things" are ready. I'm going to leave this decision up to you.

Let's think about this for a second. What happened the last time you slept with a guy you really liked who you just met? If that worked out for you, and everything is happily ever after, then who am I to judge? If sleeping with someone on a first date has not worked out for you in the past, then chances are it's time to try something different.

I want you to remember the date as being a good experience for both people. Just relax and be yourself; there is nothing more attractive than someone who's comfortable in his own skin. Eat, laugh, and tell some embarrassing stories about yourself. Ask questions about family, childhood, or anything that was not discussed during the phone discussions. Pick up on a topic from the meet-and-greet that you guys didn't finish talking about, and try not to talk about work. Have a great time, and remember to be polite to everyone while you're out (ie, cab drivers, waiters, bartenders), this says a lot about you to the person you're on a date with. Good Luck!!

Chapter Eight

SIX DEGREES OF BLAH, BLAH, BLAH

From time to time in life, we go through what I call a "Dark Period." Most of the time, this can stem from just about anything: a bad breakup, family issues, monetary problems, etc. During this time period, we still tend to meet and date people. On some levels, this may serve as a distraction from our problems, but it never works. The Dark Period also means that we are emotionally unavailable to date in the first place. We do it anyway, and many times we end up hurting people in the process.

We all deal with our painful issues in life differently. Some people are mentally stronger than others. Have you ever had a friend you haven't seen in a while, and you say "OMG, how have you been? I've not seen you in, like, forever"? More than likely, this person may be dealing with an ordeal in life that causes him to be reclusive. Other people cope during a Dark Period with a range of activities, from excessive sexual partners to drinking to drug use; this just numbs the problems we don't want to address. The problem with these habit-forming activities is that it creates a snowball effect, because you do more of it to avoid dealing with your issues that caused the "Dark Period" to begin with. I believe this creates a nasty dating cycle that must be stopped.

So what can you do if you meet someone you can clearly see has potential but who seems to be going through a Dark Period? First, make sure you can identify that this person is going through something. Just listen to him carefully and don't probe with questions; allow him to vent and express his feelings. Most people don't open up right away, but I find it's easier just to wait for any information you want to come out of his mouth in time. If you see this guy is a good person who's going through some things, then dating is probably not his priority, but make it clear that you can provide a good ear if it's ever needed.

I've had my share of dating woes when it came to the Dark Period types. I've always felt like I could help, fix everything, or just see them through their dark cloud, but I've been wrong over and over again. There is no amount of encouragement or support that can be given to mitigate someone else's issue, to make him a suitable person to date. I will say again, sometimes people just need to vent to someone—and surprisingly, this can help out a lot, so it's good to be this someone.

Most of us are good people, and we all have our ups and downs in life. The good thing about the Dark Period is that it's temporary, like a dark cloud that passes in the sky. We eventually deal with whatever issues we have, and just like any bad storm, there are always casualties. The causalities are often the people we may have met or attempted to date. For the most part, these people may have been enthusiastic about getting to know you better, and I'm sure a lot of you in a Dark Period sent that shit straight to hell. So what happens next? I personally believe this creates a ripple effect for great guys who may have been open to dating but became turned off because they opened themselves up to someone in a "Dark Period." I understand how it feels, trying to date someone you clearly see is a good guy but you know isn't ready. Also, I have been the guy who hurt innocent bystanders, because I shouldn't have been trying to date during my "DP." I learned a lot, as I see when I reflect on a chain of events that has taken place during my dating experiences.

Like I said earlier, it's like a storm that passes. Now the cleanup has to take place within yourself; if possible, make amends with some of your victims. You would think this topic would be common sense, but it's not. Part of moving on from your "DP" is trying to do some damage control. Even if the person you're reaching out to doesn't want to hear anything you have to say, at least you know you tried.

When you do get that one person's ear, explain to him the truth about whatever happened, and—without giving too much detail—share with him a piece of what you were going through. Now, I know some of you shady bitches are thinking, *Why would I do this?* Well, even if the person is still mad about whatever happened, over time, he would have to respect what you were attempting to do. Quite honestly, it's the adult thing to do also; this will relieve that person from thinking it was him who cause a problem. This can also begin to stop some of the bad "dating ripple effects." (We've all been in this position; we met a guy, had a date, thought it went well, and then the person just disappeared. Then you think, *Was it something I said?*) By the way, you never know how this will play itself out in the future in your favor.

Here is another example: You meet a guy, and everything is going great. You're spending a lot of time with each other and having dinner, going to the theater and for long walks in the park. You're having endless phone conversations into the early morning. At that point, the level of dating escalates to the two of you spending time in each other's apartments, spending the night and weekends. Then it's time to meet whoever is important to the person you're dating. This can be anybody—friends, family, or whoever; you will start meeting them one by one. Then the day will come when a big dinner party or get-together is planned, and this is an opportunity to get everyone acquainted.

All of this nervous energy starts to form, because we all know that the opinions of loved ones about the person we are dating are a big deal. So everything has to be perfect about your appearance, your manners, all of it. Then you show up to the event or gathering, and this happens:

Dater 1: "Hey, baby, I want you to meet my best friend."
Dater 2: "Sure, where is he?"
Best Friend: "Turn around. I'm right here, *bitch.*"
Dater 2: "Oh, hey, how you been?"
Best Friend: "Whatever. Excuse me, me and my best friend need to talk. Be right back."

This can go a few different ways, but clearly the best friend has a problem with who his friend is dating. The story begins; Dater 1 realizes he is dating a guy who's done some really cruel and mean things to his friend (during your Dark Period). So what do you think will happen to this great guy you met, if you were Dater 2? Chances are, Dater 1 might side with his BFF, and all the time spent getting to know someone may have been wasted.

Now let's think about this. Dater 2 clearly met the BFF during his "DP." What if Dater 2 went back and spoke to this BFF and explained some things that were going on at that time and apologized? You get the picture. I'm sure that Dater 1 and his BFF would be having a different discussion, while Dater 2 is waiting.

Being upfront and making an attempt to rectify any wrongs is a strong sign of one's maturity level. Don't we all want to date someone who knows the right and wrong way to handle a situation? Be *kind and respectful* to everyone; you and everyone else deserve it. I'm going to say this again: You never know who knows who. Therefore, being mean or hurtful to the wrong guy will always come back to bite you in the ass. This can be applied across the board, not just with dating, but with job interviews, business meetings; hell, I've seen an apartment listing not shown to a person just because he screwed someone over.

The reason I mention the Dark Period is because many (but not all) Gay men go through a self-destructive phase when coping with hurtful things in life. This may stem from Gay men dealing with rejection from all angles at an early age, well into our adulthood, from our families or friends, from society, and worse, from ourselves. I personally believe this creates an eternal sense of never feeling completely adequate. This may lead to overcompensating with our careers, finances, relationships, and so on. This can create a lot of pressure to keep up appearances to hold everything together. Ultimately, I find that a lot of people put together a house of cards in life that can easily be torn down by removing one card. Then, as an individual, you have a mess to clean up from the foundation up. While this person is picking up the pieces of his life, people who are in the way can get hurt in the process.

Most self destructive people in the Dark Period are too messy or too high even to know if they hurt someone in the process of their messiness. What's worse is a lot of them who may be aware don't care who they hurt, because they're hurting and can't see past their own pain. If you know for a fact that you're in a Dark Period in life, try to refrain from dating until all of these issues are back in order. For you desperate Gay men, if you meet a man, and he is clearly not datable because he is in a "DP," just put the dick down and walk away. Save yourself the future heartache for both parties. Remember, guys, just use the Golden Rule: Treat others the way you want to be treated . . . that's it.

Chapter Nine

I FOUND SOMEONE...I THINK

Now you have done all of the dating, and you've decided to focus your energy on someone you feel is special. This is always a relief in a way, because you can stop the "dating wheel" for a while and explore this opportunity. In this chapter, we're going to cover some prerequisites before you go too far too soon. Below is a conversation between two best friends in the whole world:

Gay 1: "Hey, I have something to tell you."

Gay 2: "What is it now, hooker?"

Gay 1: "Well, I met this guy, and we spent four hours last night on the phone . . . . We have so much in common with each other."

Gay 2: "You know I have heard this shit like twelve times this year, and it's only March."

Gay 1: "You're just jealous because you never got rid of that twenty-year-old baby fat and can't meet anybody."

Gay 2: "Please, you better go do something about your golden smile."

Gay 1: "Are we still on for drinks later?"

Gay 2: "Sure, don't be late, tramp."

I know I'm wrong about the skit above, but how many times have we called our friends each time we meet a nice guy? Nonetheless, it's a good feeling when you met a potential guy and there is a mutual attraction. I believe a lot of it is due to the curiosity about someone's life and sharing experiences and the possibilities for the future. The more you find you have in common with this guy, the more you really start to think you've found someone perfect for you. In most cases, you more than likely met the perfect guy, but so much information is not covered in the beginning, so I want to focus on that for a bit.

Isn't it funny that so many things are dedicated to the same topic over and over—love? Countless books, movies, and songs are written about love and heartbreak. It's the one thing that I believe connects people all over the world, regardless of race or creed. This emotion crosses language barriers, and a love song can still move you, even if you don't understand the words; the pain or joy is always recognizable. Everyone you meet for the rest of your life will have a story to tell you about this very topic, love.

For the gays, we have a much higher turnover rate in the love department than most people. We can meet a guy, and within a matter of weeks, we're in a new relationship. Yes, it's just as silly as it sounds, but it continues to happen every hookup . . . I mean every day.

Fine, I was trying to avoid this topic and keep everything tasteful, but that wouldn't be real, would it? So it's time to talk about "the hookup factor." I know I didn't factor this into an earlier chapter, but I didn't want to have my book go take an STD test right away.

I have to put this out there, and some people aren't going to like this. Let's face it: Most of the time, these fast relationships are spawned out of a hot, sweaty night of unbridled passion. So, boys and boy-girls, what does this tell us? Yes, we base a lot of our relationships on good sex. Come on, people! I mean, just because the sex is good doesn't mean you are meant to be together! Now, don't get me wrong; sex is an important factor, but it *cannot* be the foundation of any relationship.

Let's take a poll. How many relationships that you know were based on sex have worked out? If for some godforsaken way, it did work out, how many of them are healthy relationships? Exactly! True, some people have met this way, and everything seems to fall right into place. Trust me, those people are lucky. Now that I got that off my chest, we can move on.

When things begin to get serious with a guy you have been seeing, I call this the honeymoon phase. You want to be around him all the time; you become consumed with thinking about him. If you look straight into his eyes, you get that nervous energy in your stomach. You begin texting each other throughout the day, when your ass should be working, calling each other on your damn lunch breaks. You never miss a phone call from him. The sex is extra passionate because it's new; each time, it gets better and better because you're learning what turns each other on, and emotions start to run high. Your life feels like there could never be a rainy day.

During this honeymoon phase, we are a bit blinded by our new emotions, and we do not always see everything clearly. So I will point some things out that are normally missed during this period of a new relationship. I want everyone to take a second and think about your last serious relationship or someone you dated for a while, and it didn't work out. Rewind all the way to the beginning, when you first met that person. You'll remember that you were in your honeymoon phase, and everything was like springtime and butterflies with glitter on them like you were in the damn Magic Kingdom, right? Or was it?

At the end of a relationship, we can always point out any issues and problems as clearly as our eyes can spot a guy in gym shorts with no underwear. Those problems and issues were always there. We were blinded by glitter and shit during our honeymoon phase and ignored these things. We can always rewind to the beginning and find red flags that were very small at first. As you come out of the honeymoon phase, the red flags become bigger and bigger. Depending on how long you were with that person, it will look like Six Flags toward the end.

I want you to enjoy your honeymoon, but make sure your reading glasses are on. You need to pay close attention for any little flags that may pop up with this guy. Sure, no one is perfect, but you have to know what you can and cannot deal with—and if you think for a second you can fix or change it, you're wrong! For example, I mentioned this in an earlier chapter: I won't tolerate disrespect from someone I'm dating or involved with. Another deal-breaker for me is bad communication skills. If we cannot have an adult conversation about a problem or our feelings, then we have a huge problem. You can only fix superficial things about a person, but you cannot change the core of who an individual is. Trust me, I have tried, and I fell on my face each time.

Now, when you find one red flag in the beginning, think about that flag and fast-forward a month, a year, three years, and think about what the flags could turn into. Again, ask yourself if you can live with whatever that issue may or may not be. I would recommend making sure you see a pattern with the flag before you make a final decision.

Let's talk about that word, *love*. I want you to take a minute and think about what love and being in love mean to you. When you have your answer thought out, make sure you remember it, because this is going to be one of many questions you will want to answer about your potential partner. Well, I wouldn't really call them questions. It is more along the lines of one's definitions of words. A lot of definitions of certain words will give you an idea of where someone is morally. Below is a discussion with one of my exes about his night out and why we need to understand what certain things means to people.

Me: "Hey, baby, did you have a good time tonight?"

Him: "Indeed I did. I really needed to get out the house."

Me: "I'm glad you had a good time. Did you eat?"

Him: "Yeah, I grabbed something after I left the bar. I'm tired. I'm just going to go to sleep."

Me: "Okay, me too. I will be in there in a minute. Did anything interesting happen?"

Him: "Nah, same old same old."

Me: "Cool."

[THE NEXT MORNING]

Me: "Wake your ass up!"

Him: "What happened?"

Me: "What the hell is this? I found this on my way to the bathroom."

Him: "It's a number I got from a guy I met last night."

Me: "Really! So when I asked you about your night, you left this part out. So you lied about it?"

Him: "I didn't lie to you. I just didn't tell you about it."

This is when I knew this was not going to work out between him and me. We had two different definitions of what a lie was. He felt that if he didn't tell me about something, it wasn't the same as a lie. To me, withholding information about anything is the same as a lie.

Here are a few examples of what you're going to ask, and share your answers with someone you're dating.

What's a lie to you?
What do you consider the truth?
What's cheating to you?
What's love to you?
Loyalty?
Communication?

The answers to these questions give you a bit of insight into a person's view on these core relationship or long-term dating values. You can keep adding to this list if you'd like, but I find that people don't talk about these topics when they first meet someone because they are in the honeymoon phase. I'm sure if they did, this could make building a bond between two people easier. Maybe this could prevent some unneeded heartache as well.

I like to look at someone I'm dating as if I would make him a friend—well, a friend I would have sex with, but what I mean by that is when we pick our friends it is usually for a few good reasons. We have great discussions about current events, we might work out together, we have common business interests; I can go on and on, but ultimately we are friends with people who share a common moral ground with us. So this shouldn't change when you meet someone you want to spend more time with.

Also, if the morals are in place, make sure there are some shared interests. For example, I love British literature, Charles Dickens or anything Elizabethan. I love watching foreign films on the weekend. I've only dated two guys who shared these interests, and I found that we had a lot of other similar interests that are considered uncommon for Gay men in general. So try to talk about interests that only really close friends know about you with this person you're spending time with. This will give a lot of insight into what kind of person you are. You may be surprised to find how many people are quietly into the same things you enjoy, and this may spark a deeper connection between the two.

Let's take a few minutes to think about our grandparents or the old couple who lives in your building or neighborhood and can say, "We have been together for thirty years." I always find it amazing to be able to say that sentence. Thinking about these people can take you back in time to a society that was very different than ours today. Men were gentlemen, and women were ladies. A lady had to be called on and properly asked out on a date, and a high level of respect was demanded from the start.

Many years ago, respect was just the minimal standard for a man meeting any woman (even prostitutes), and many women held themselves in high regard. This forced men to be gentlemen; even if a man was not one, he still needed to play the part. Also, the word "courting" actually meant just that: Time was taken out for a man and a woman to genuinely get to know each other before anything happened, even a kiss.

Let's think about this. I had a conversation with a Greek cab driver, and we were talking a bit about relationships. He asked me a question: "Do you ever notice that a lot of older couples that have been together a long time shared either the same or similar cultural backgrounds?" I had to think for a minute, and then I agreed with him. How many movies have we seen where an Italian man or woman fell in love with an Irish person, and it was considered taboo? Consider another example of two people from different backgrounds falling in love, *West Side Story*: Why was it such a problem?

This is just my opinion. Could it be that if you shared the same or similar backgrounds a lot of the same moral values were already established between a man and woman? Let's fast-forward to today's blended society. How many people have a family tree that looks like a pack of Skittles? A lot of us! So what changes when you have many cultures mixed together? Does this make it harder to meet someone who matches some of the morals you were brought up with?

I have a theory. I believe the key to a successful relationship is having similar moral values. Granted, you're not going to meet someone who matches everything, but I'm referring to the values that are most important to you. Integrity, selflessness, and ethics are just a few that are important to me. The hard part is pinpointing these details in people; a lot of these things can come up during the course of getting to know someone special.

Lastly, keep your lonely Dark Period friends out of your business and your new relationship. The Dark Period people are bitter and lonely and don't want to see anyone else happy right now. So keep the information about your newfound love on a need-to-know basis, and keep things easy-breezy; there's no need to rush into anything. Enjoy the courtship of dating. For some reason, I find that titles make people nervous. When you assign titles too quickly to a new relationship, it always comes with responsibilities and accountability. It can cause some people who are unready for that to pull back from a potentially good thing too soon, out of fear.

As Gay men, we don't date long enough. You'll be surprised what you can learn about a person if you date them for six months or longer. Try to put your ego away while dating. Don't be afraid to express how you feel about someone. If the guy you're dating is the one expressing his feelings, try to meet him halfway. One more thing to keep in mind while dating: if it's not working out, don't waste each other's time. Let it go, and get back out there and start looking for another special guy you may be more compatible with. Remember to try to remain friends with someone you dated, because you may run into him again and again.

Chapter Ten

THE WHOLE DAMN POINT!

You would think that if you are living in a city like New York or any other large city, the Gay population would be bigger, but it is always very small. At some point, if you live in any city long enough, the Gay community kind of turns into a big, dysfunctional family. We know how family can be; you will always have one side of a family that doesn't speak to another side for whatever reason. Normally, the family squabbles are not very important, but we all have the same kind of family, one way or another.

For instance, we're all familiar with the following family members: a drug addict, the family whore, the married couple who are just keeping up appearances (but you really know they are both cheating on each other with every Tom, Dick, and Harry, Jason, Jose, Ian, Peter, Derrick, James, and Joseph). Then you have the "fixers" in the family, the problem-solvers. The fixers are always settling family fights, helping out with monetary issues, or just giving advice. A lot of times, the fixers have to deal with a lot of resentment from family members, because sometimes people don't want to hear the truth.

Gay Men pretty much have the same family structure; a lot of times, Gay men recreate a family unit they may or may not have had within their own family. Clearly, people have become a bit more tolerant of dealing with Gay family or friends in recent years, but it doesn't change the fact that Gay men have picked their own family. Over the years, the nature of any family starts to change, and people tend to go off and do their own thing. Sometimes this is a great thing, and other times it can be trouble. A lot of people I know—including me—are guilty of severing ties with people. I mean, hell, we're good at it because we are quick to cut our real family off without blinking an eye. A group of Gay friends/family can go through that over and over for years.

When you think about it, love does not know any distance or boundaries. Just because you don't see all of your family all the time, it doesn't stop you from loving them. Even if you're mad at them, you still care about what happens to them. Well, the Gay family is the same way; years and distance and lack of communication do not keep us from continuing to love one another.

Now let's talk about the troubled souls I mentioned earlier. The family whore, the drug abuser, the alcoholic, and the fake happy couple are all part of our real and chosen family. In my opinion, these are people who may be struggling with issues; they need to dig deeper to the core of their problem . . . and fix it! I'm also finding that all of these problems have the same thing in common: self-destructive behavior. How does one overcome something like this? Most of these actions are habit-forming, so they've developed over a long period of time. This means that just as we remembered the beginning of any relationship that didn't work out, we rewind to the beginning, we have to do the same in this case. This is the question that still needs to be asked: "When was the last time I felt completely happy?"

This question of happiness may be deeper than you know. When I asked myself that question, I had trouble answering this question. On my own I could not explain why I didn't know the last time I was completely happy. Don't get me wrong, I have a lot of happy moments in life. I'm referring to when you didn't feel like there was a void in your life. I worked with a therapist on several areas of my life, from childhood to adulthood and traced the causes and effects of a lot of things that took place that I didn't fully understand. During therapy I was able to come full circle about my life's events and was able to say yes I'm happy . . . now.

It's funny—our childhood is so short, but it can affect our adult lives for much longer than the time we were kids. Sometimes we have to go back in time and forgive people for anything hurtful that happened to us.

It's important first to acknowledge what took place and make peace with that. Then we can keep working on these past issues until we come to the present day. The goal is to look in the mirror and say, "Damn, I'm the shit," not only because you look and feel amazing, but because you have overcome hardship and adversity, and you're still here. Then you can say to yourself, "I love you," and practice loving yourself.

With practicing to love yourself, you will watch any self-destructive behavior slowly come to an end. You will not tolerate disrespect from anyone, because you respect yourself. You won't take lies from anyone, because you're true to yourself. And if you're in a relationship that is emotionally dead, you will separate yourself, because you will know you deserve better. You will no longer look for someone to make you a whole person, because you repaired the half that was damaged. You will continue taking steps to being happy—because you're happy. You will find the things in life that bring you joy as an individual. Your health and well-being will be your top priorities in life.

I truly believe that whatever doesn't kill you makes you stronger, and life is supposed to have obstacles, but it's how we deal with obstacles that separates the strong from the weak. Also, our real and chosen families will always be our safety net if we need it, but we should never rely solely on them. Then we have the men we meet along our journey in life. These are the men we're dating, and spending precious time getting to know. Because a lot of us have seen the "Dark Period," either in ourselves or others, we will recognize it when we see it and know how to avoid it.

We will go out in public with confidence, because we are sure of ourselves, and look for other like-minded individuals.

At the end of the day, we are all men, and they say it's a man's world. Understanding each other as men is important when it comes to dating. We need to move away from being a superficial community when it comes to meeting people. The beauty of any person can never be found in his physical attributes; it's in one's heart and mind. Also, we have to know what we want in everything we do. That's the first step to getting what you want in life: knowing what you want! I don't care if it's choosing career goals, picking where you want to live, deciding to be debt-free . . . anything! Make a decision about what you want, and have goals to make it happen. This also applies to dating; know what kind of man you're looking for. There is a huge chance that he is looking for you too! I personally believe that two strong-minded men who are emotionally and physically healthy can conquer anything together. Never give up on what you deserve, and never just settle for what's in front of you. I want every Gay man who is interested in dating to use this book as a guide to sort out some of the bad apples. Have discussions about some of the topics discussed here. If you don't agree with everything, it's okay; I want people to have a dialogue about these things. Let's see what happens. I'm also interested in hearing any stories you would like to share.

I'm going to end on this note using a quote from an iconic 1958 movie called *Auntie Mame.* Patrick Dennis wrote a book that was later turned into this movie starring Rosalind Russell.

"Life is a banquet, and most poor suckers are starving to death. So live, live, live!"

So go date, have fun, create new experiences, and explore whatever the city you're in has to offer. And *live!* With an open mind and an open heart, you will find the man you're looking for.